NFC EAST

BY ELLEN LABRECQUE

★ Dallas Cowboys ★ New York Giants ★ Philadelphia Eagles ★ Washington Redskins ★

Published by The Child's World®
1980 Lookout Drive
Mankato, MN 56003-1705
800-599-READ
www.childsworld.com

The Child's World®: Mary Berendes, Publishing Director
The Design Lab: Kathleen Petelinsek, Design
Editorial Directions, Inc.:
Pam Mamsch and E. Russell Primm, Project Managers

Photographs ©: Robbins Photography

Library of Congress Cataloging-in-Publication Data
Labrecque, Ellen.
  NFC East / by Ellen LaBrecque.
    p. cm. Includes bibliographical references and index.
  ISBN 978-1-60973-131-1 (library reinforced : alk. paper)
  1. National Football Conference—Juvenile literature.
  2. Football—East (U. S.)—Juvenile literature. I. Title.
  GV950.7.L3 2011
  796.332'640973—dc22   2011007152

Printed in the United States of America
Mankato, MN
May, 2011
PA02093

TABLE OF
CONTENTS

NFC
EAST

First Season: 1960
NFL Championships: 5
Colors: Blue, White, and
   Silver
Mascot: Rowdy the
   Cowboy

★

DALLAS
COWBOYS

TRUE BLUE FANS!

The Dallas Cowboys are the most popular team in the NFL. There are eight good reasons for that: The Cowboys have played in the Super Bowl eight times. That is the most of any NFL team! (They won five and lost three.)

The Cowboys are also the only NFL team to record 20 winning seasons in a row (1966–1985). They only missed the playoffs twice in those years (1974 and 1984).

Dallas joined the NFL in 1960 as an **expansion team**. They had a slow start. In fact, they did not win a game at all that season (0–11–1). After many exciting years, the past **decade** has seen the Cowboys fall from their mighty horse. They have only made the playoffs four times in the past ten seasons. But they are on the upswing again. Their best year was in 2009, when they finished first in their division with an 11–5 record.

Running back Emmitt Smith was the first NFL player ever to rush for more than 1,000 yards 11 seasons in a row.

HOME FIELD

The Cowboys play their home games at Cowboys
Stadium in Arlington, Texas. It was completed
in 2009 and is the largest domed stadium in the
world. It also has the largest high-definition video
screen in the world. It stretches from one 20-yard
line to the other 20-yard line.

BIG DAYS

★ The Cowboys dominated the 1990s. In fact, they
   won five straight NFC East Division titles and
   three Super Bowls from 1992 to 1996.
★ The Cowboys' most recent Super Bowl title came
   on January 28, 1996. They beat the Pittsburgh
   Steelers 27–17.

Cowboys Stadium covers 73 acres (30 hectares) of land.

SUPERSTARS!

★

THEN

Troy Aikman, quarterback: led the Cowboys to three Super Bowl titles
Michael Irvin, wide receiver: gained more than
1,000 yards in seven of his 12 seasons
Emmitt Smith, running back: NFL's all-time rushing leader (18,355 yards)
Roger Staubach, quarterback: led Dallas to five
NFC titles and two Super Bowl rings

★

NOW

Terence Newman, cornerback: loaded with speed, and
named to the Pro Bowl in 2008 and 2010
Tony Romo, quarterback: gutsy leader who makes daring passes
DeMarcus Ware, linebacker: terrorizes opposing quarterbacks

★

STAT LEADERS

(All-time team leaders*)
Passing Yards: Troy Aikman, 32,942
Rushing Yards: Emmitt Smith, 17,162
Receiving Yards: Michael Irvin, 11,904
Touchdowns: Emmitt Smith, 164
Interceptions: Mel Renfro, 52

★

TIMELINE

(*Through 2010 season.)

1960	1967	1970	1971	1977
Dallas Cowboys join the NFL as an expansion team.	Cowboys lose to the Green Bay Packers 21–17 in the NFL "Ice Bowl" Championship.	Dallas loses to the Baltimore Colts in Super Bowl V, 16–13.	Cowboys defeat the Miami Dolphins 24–3 to win their first Super Bowl title.	Cowboys beat the Denver Broncos 27–10 to captur their second Super Bowl

Tony Romo was a backup quarterback for three seasons before becoming the recordbreaker he is today.

1992
Cowboys defeat the Buffalo Bills 52–17 for their third title.

1993
Dallas beats the Buffalo Bills 30–13 in the Super Bowl for the second season in a row.

1995
Dallas earns its fifth Super Bowl title by beating the Pittsburgh Steelers 27–17.

2009
Cowboys win their twenty-first Division Championship.

First Season: 1925
NFL Championships: 7
Colors: Dark Blue, Red, Gray, and White
Mascot: None

★

NEW YORK
GIANTS

LONG LIVE THE GIANTS

Few teams can match the tradition of the New York Giants. They joined the NFL in 1925 and won four titles in the pre–Super Bowl **era**. And they have won three Super Bowl titles since the big game began in 1967. Their last Super Bowl victory was in 2008.

The Giants have a long history of dominating on defense. In the 1980s, their defense was nicknamed the Big Blue Wrecking Crew. The **franchise** holds the NFL record for most seasons leading the league with fewest points allowed (11 seasons).

Wide receiver Steve Smith set a team record with 107 receptions in the 2009 season.

HOME FIELD

The Giants play their home games at the New Meadowlands Stadium in East Rutherford, New Jersey. The 2010 season was the first one in the new stadium. The Giants share the stadium with the New York Jets. They are the only two NFL teams to share their home turf.

BIG DAYS

★ The 1980s and early 1990s were powerful years for the Giants. Bill Parcells was their coach. The 1986 Giants are considered one of the best NFL teams ever. They went 14–2 for the season and won their first Super Bowl title, defeating the Denver Broncos 39–20. They scored 30 points in the second half—a Super Bowl record.

★ The Giants won their third Super Bowl title in 2007. They upset the New England Patriots, who had won 18 straight games and were playing for a perfect season.

New Meadowlands Stadium seats more than 80,000 fans.

SUPERSTARS!

★

THEN

Frank Gifford, halfback: starred on offense and defense
Phil Simms, quarterback: threw for 268 yards and three
touchdowns in Super Bowl XXI
Lawrence Taylor, linebacker: quarterbacks feared his speed
and powerful tackling ability

★

NOW

Eli Manning, quarterback: one of the strongest arms in the league
Steve Smith, wide receiver: demands defensive double teams
Justin Tuck, defensive end: team leader and tops at forcing **fumbles**

★

STAT LEADERS
(All-time team leaders*)
Passing Yards: Phil Simms, 33,462
Rushing Yards: Tiki Barber, 10,449
Receiving Yards: Amani Toomer, 9,497
Touchdowns: Frank Gifford, 78
Interceptions: Emlen Tunnell, 74

★

(*Through 2010 season.)

TIMELINE

1925	1927	1938	1970
New York Giants join the NFL.	The Giants finish with the league's best record, 11-1-1.	New York becomes the first NFL team to win two championship games, beating the Green Bay Packers 23-17.	Running back Ron Johnson becomes the team's first 1,000-yard season rusher (1,027).

Quarterback Eli Manning was chosen as the first overall pick by the San Diego Chargers in the 2004 NFL Draft.

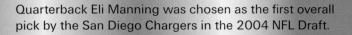

1986
The Giants win their first Super Bowl, defeating the Denver Broncos 39–20.

1989
Giants win their second NFC East championship in four seasons.

1991
Giants upset the Buffalo Bills 20–19 for their second Super Bowl title in five seasons.

2007
Giants shock the undefeated New England Patriots by beating them 17–14 to win Super Bowl XLII.

First Season: 1933
NFL Championships: 3
Colors: Midnight Green,
Black, Charcoal,
Silver, and White
Mascot: Swoop

★

PHILADELPHIA
EAGLES

E-A-G-L-E-S! EAGLES

The Philadelphia Eagles have some of the loudest, craziest, and most loyal fans in the league. The "Iggles" joined the NFL in 1933. They replaced a Philadelphia-based team called the Frankford Yellow Jackets. They did not have a winning season until ten years later.

Philly has appeared in the Super Bowl twice (1980 and 2004), but they have never won the big game. They did win three league titles in the pre–Super Bowl era.

Kicker David Akers has been selected to the Pro Bowl five times in his 12-year NFL career.

HOME FIELD

The Eagles play their home games at the Lincoln Financial Field in South Philadelphia. The 2003 season was the first one played in the "Linc." During the first two seasons, the stadium even had a jail that housed out-of-control fans!

BIG DAYS

★ Philadelphia has been one of the best teams in football in the last decade. Under head coach Andy Reid, the team has had just one losing record since 2000 and has made the playoffs in eight of those seasons.

★ In January 2009, Philadelphia beat the defending Super Bowl champs, the New York Giants, to advance to their fifth NFC championship game in eight years. Quarterback Donovan McNabb led the charge.

The 67,594-seat Lincoln Financial Field cost $512 million to build.

SUPERSTARS!

★

THEN

Chuck Bednarik, linebacker: last player to play both offense and defense

Donovan McNabb, quarterback: the Eagles' all-time leader in career wins, passing yards, and passing touchdowns

Reggie White, defensive end: the jersey of "the Minister of Defense" is retired

★

NOW

David Akers, kicker: holds the NFL record for points in a single decade

LeSean McCoy, running back: set the team's rookie rushing record

Asante Samuel, cornerback: the king of **interceptions**

★

STAT LEADERS

(All-time team leaders*)

Passing Yards: Donovan McNabb, 32,873

Rushing Yards: Wilbert Montgomery, 6,538

Receiving Yards: Harold Carmichael, 8,978

Touchdowns: Harold Carmichael, 79

Interceptions: Brian Dawkins, 34

★

(*Through 2010 season.)

TIMELINE

1933	1943	1948	1949	1960
Philadelphia Eagles join the NFL.	Eagles **merge** with the Pittsburgh Steelers to form the Steagles; the merger ends at the end of the season.	Eagles win their first NFL championship, defeating the Chicago Cardinals 7–0.	Philly wins its second NFL title over the Los Angeles Rams 14–0.	Eagles beat the Gree Packers 17–13 for t third NFL title.

In the 2010 season, LeSean McCoy had more receptions than any other running back in the NFL.

1980
Philly plays in its first Super Bowl, losing to the Oakland Raiders 27-10.

2001
Eagles soar to their first NFC East division title since 1988.

2004
Eagles head to the Super Bowl for the first time in 24 years; they lose to the New England Patriots 24-21.

2008
Philly appears in its fifth NFC Championship title game in a decade, losing to the Arizona Cardinals 32-25.

First Season: 1932
NFL Championships: 5
Colors: Burgundy and
Mustard
Mascot: None

★

WASHINGTON
REDSKINS

WONDERFUL IN WASHINGTON

Don't talk smack about the Washington Redskins. Skins fans have broken the NFL's mark for single-season attendance eight years in a row. They have also been rewarded for their unfailing faith. Washington has won five NFL championships, including three Super Bowl titles. The Skins played in two more Super Bowl games, which they lost.

The Washington franchise began in Boston and was named the Braves. In 1933, they changed their name to the Boston Redskins, in honor of their head coach, William "Lone Star" Dietz, an American Indian. The team moved to Washington, D.C., in 1937.

Wide receiver Santana Moss led the league in receptions and receiving yards for five consecutive seasons from 2005 to 2009.

HOME FIELD

The Redskins play their home games at FedEx Field in Landover, Maryland. It is the largest **venue** in the NFL and can hold 91,704 fans! The next-biggest stadium is the one shared by the New York Giants and the New York Jets. It holds 10,000 less people than FedEx Field does.

BIG DAYS

★ The Redskins' history is highlighted by two major periods. The first was from 1936 to 1945. The team appeared in six NFL championship games and won two of them.

★ The Skins also dominated from 1982 to 1991. They won four NFC titles and won the Super Bowl three of the four times they played.

It took 17 months and $250 million to complete construction on FedEx Field.

SUPERSTARS!

★

THEN

Sammy Baugh, quarterback: Slingin' Sammy was one of the first QBs to excel at the passing game
Art Monk, wide receiver: one of the NFL's all-time leading receivers
John Riggins, running back: a workhorse runner who delivered the tough yards in the tough games

★

NOW

DeAngelo Hall, cornerback: smothers the fastest receivers in the league
Donovan McNabb, quarterback: a longtime Philly star, he has one of the most powerful arms in the game
Santana Moss, wide receiver: a slippery speedster

★

STAT LEADERS

(All-time team leaders*)
Passing Yards: Joe Theismann, 25,206
Rushing Yards: John Riggins, 7,472
Receiving Yards: Art Monk, 12,028
Touchdowns: Charley Taylor, 90
Interceptions: Darrell Green, 54

★

(*Through 2010 season.)

TIMELINE

1932
Team is established as the Boston Braves.

1937
They become the Washington Redskins and win their first NFL championship, defeating the Chicago Bears 28-21.

1942
Skins win their second NFL championship, beating the Chicago Bears 14-6.

1972
Washington plays in its fi Super Bowl but loses to t Miami Dolphins 14-7.

Veteran quarterback Donovan McNabb played 11 seasons with the Philadelphia Eagles before joining the Redskins in 2010.

1982
Redskins win their first Super Bowl title by defeating the Miami Dolphins 27–17.

1983
Washington loses the Super Bowl to the Los Angeles Raiders 38–9.

1987
Redskins win second their Super Bowl title by beating the Denver Broncos 42–10.

1991
Redskins win their third Super Bowl title by beating the Buffalo Bills 37–24.

2006
Washington makes the playoffs for the first time since 1999.

STAT
STUFF

★

NFC EAST DIVISION STATISTICS*

Team	All-Time Record (W-L-T)	NFL Titles (Most Recent)	Times in NFL Playoffs
Dallas Cowboys	439–321–6	5 (1996)	30
New York Giants	636–524–33	7 (2008)	30
Philadelphia Eagles	509–539–26	3 (1960)	23
Washington Redskins	547–515–27	5 (1991)	22

★

NFC EAST DIVISION CHAMPIONSHIPS (MOST RECENT)

Dallas Cowboys . . . 20 (2009)
New York Giants . . . 7 (2008)
Philadelphia Eagles . . . 8 (2010)
Washington Redskins . . . 7 (1999)

★

(*Through 2010 season.)

Position Key:
QB: Quarterback
RB: Running back
WR: Wide receiver
C: Center
T: Tackle
G: Guard
CB: Cornerback
LB: Linebacker
DE: Defensive end
HB: Halfback
S: Safety
FB: Fullback
TE: Tight end
DT: Defensive tack
OT: Offensive tack
DB: Defensive back

NFC EAST PRO FOOTBALL HALL OF FAME MEMBERS

Dallas Cowboys

Herb Adderley, CB
Troy Aikman, QB
Mike Ditka, TE
Tony Dorsett, RB
Bob Hayes, WR
Michael Irvin, WR
Tom Landry, Coach
Bob Lilly, DT
Mel Renfro, CB, S
Deion Sanders, CB
Tex Schramm,
  Administrator
Emmitt Smith, RB
Roger Staubach,
  QB
Randy White, DT
Rayfield Wright, T

New York Giants

Morris (Red)
  Badgro, DE
Roosevelt Brown,
  OT
Harry Carson, LB
Larry Csonka, FB
Ray Flaherty,
  Coach
Benny Friedman,
  QB
Frank Gifford, HB
Mel Hein, C
Robert (Cal)
  Hubbard, T
Sam Huff, LB
Alphonse (Tuffy)
  Leemans, RB
Tim Mara, Owner
Wellington Mara,
  Owner
Steve Owen,
  Coach, T
Andy Robustelli,
  DE
Ken Strong, HB
Fran Tarkenton, QB
Lawrence Taylor,
  LB
Y. A. Tittle, QB
Emlen Tunnell,
  DB
Arnie
  Weinmeister, DT

Philadelphia Eagles

Chuck Bednarik, C,
  LB
Bert Bell,
  Administrator,
  Owner
Bob (Boomer)
  Brown, T
Bill Hewitt, DE
Sonny Jurgensen,
  QB
Ollie Matson, HB
Tommy
  McDonald, WR
Earle (Greasy)
  Neale, Coach
Pete Pihos, DE
Jim Ringo, C
Norm Van
  Brocklin, QB
Steve Van Buren,
  HB
Reggie White, DE
Alex
  Wojciechowicz,
  C, LB

Washington Redskins

George Allen,
  Coach
Cliff Battles, HB
Sammy Baugh, QB
Bill Dudley, HB
Albert Glen (Turk)
  Edwards, T
Ray Flaherty,
  Coach
Joe Gibbs, Coach
Darrell Green, CB
Russ Grimm, G
Ken Houston, S
Sam Huff, LB
Chris Hanburger
Sonny Jurgensen,
  QB
Paul Krause, S
George Preston
  Marshall, Founder,
  Administrator
Wayne Millner, DE
Bobby Mitchell, WR,
  HB
Art Monk, WR
John Riggins, RB
Bruce Smith, DE
Charley Taylor, WR

NOTE: Includes players with at least three seasons with team. Players may appear with more than one team.

GLOSSARY

★

decade (DEK-ayd): a period of ten years

era (IHR-uh): a period of time marked by a certain event

expansion team (ek-SPAN-shuhn TEEM): a new team in a league of players drafted from or discarded by established league teams

franchise (FRAN-chize): the right or license of a team to call itself a certain name

fumbles (FUHM-buhlz): balls that have been dropped or lost after having been controlled

interceptions (in-tur-SEPT-shunz): the acts of a defensive player catching a pass intended for an offensive player

merge (MURJ): to blend or combine

venue (VEN-yoo): the place where certain events are held

FIND OUT MORE

★

BOOKS

Buckley, James, Jr. *Scholastic Ultimate Guide to Football*. New York: Franklin Watts, 2009.

Jacobs, Greg. *The Everything Kids' Football Book*. Avon, MA: Adams Media, 2010.

MacRae, Sloan. *The Dallas Cowboys*. New York: PowerKids Press, 2010.

MacRae, Sloan. *The New York Giants*. New York: PowerKids Press, 2011.

MacRae, Sloan. *The Philadelphia Eagles*. New York: PowerKids Press, 2011.

Stewart, Mark. *The Washington Redskins*. Chicago: Norwood House Press, 2008.

★

WEB SITES

For links to learn more about football visit

www.childsworld.com/links

Note to Parents, Teachers, and Librarians: We routinely verify our Web links to make sure they are safe and active sites. So encourage your readers to check them out!

31

INDEX

ABOUT THE AUTHOR

Ellen Labrecque has written many books for young readers on football, basketball, baseball, and other sports. Labrecque was an editor for *Sports Illustrated Kids*. She loves to watch her Philadelphia Eagles.